LAW OF ATTRACTION

HOW TO ATTRACT MONEY, LOVE, AND HAPPINESS
BY DAVID HOOPER

THE LAW OF ATTRACTION

*How to Attract Money,
Love, and Happiness*

Thanks, Anissa.

Contents

Introduction

There is a fundamental law of attraction in the universe that guides people's lives and is the underlying power behind all things. This law was expressed by Napoleon Hill when he said, "We become what we think about." This profound truth has been stated in many different languages and cultures throughout history. In the second century of the Common Era, the Roman emperor and Stoic philosopher Marcus Aurelius said "Our life is what our thoughts make it." This idea has been developed over time and has now become a central tenet in many spiritual traditions. Its truth has spread to many people and has more recently been expressed in a popular quote:

> *Watch your thoughts, for they become words.*
> *Watch your words, for they become actions.*
> *Watch your actions, for they become habits.*
> *Watch your habits, for they become character.*
> *Watch your character, for it becomes your destiny.*[1]
>
> —UNKNOWN

In relation to the law of attraction, we have extensive references to the idea of karma in the teachings of the Buddha. It is explained to us that our actions don't only have an effect in this life but in future lives and that this is the reason for our own misfortunes right this minute. If we are to ever escape the endless cycles of misfortune, we will have to change our direction and achieve an end to our sorrows.

> *If anyone says that a man or woman must reap in this life according to his present deeds, in that case there is no religious life, nor is an opportunity afforded for the entire extinction of sorrow. But if anyone says that what a man or woman reaps in this and future lives accords with his or her deeds present and past, in that case there is a religious life, and an opportunity is afforded for the entire extinction of a sorrow.[2]*
>
> — BUDDHA

In the New Testament, Christians are very familiar with the phrase "As ye sow, so shall ye reap."[3] This idea, presented to Christians and Buddhists alike, has also been presented in many other great religions on Earth and has been expounded by modern philosophers as well.

Earl Nightengale has referred to the law of attraction as "The Strangest Secret". When asked by his readers, "Why do you call it the strangest secret?" he explains that it is a secret that is really "no secret" at all. It's not because the law of attraction is hidden from view that makes it so strange. In fact, it isn't hidden. It's extremely obvious and yet nobody seems to be aware of it. "We become what we think about" is no "secret" at all and that's what makes it so strange.[4]

– PART I –

THE SCIENCE
OF ATTRACTION

*W*hen we think about attraction, we often think about the person who makes us feel the best. We think about 'being attractive' or 'having an attraction'. Everyone knows about it because attraction is often associated with individual people who we wish to emulate or "become". These people are the ones who have all the 'right' qualities; they are beautiful, intelligent or possessing a great personality. They have all the things we want in ourselves.

Attraction is a very powerful energy and yet it is often misunderstood in terms of its immense power. This is because we often limit our understanding to the manner in which we view other people. Scientists, however, say that the power of attraction is actually one of the four fundamental interactions in nature and goes much further than just a power between people. Attraction is a power in nature that can act over great distances.

According to science and other great teachings, attraction is something that affects absolutely everything in the universe. When we look back over the history of science, we remember that Newton's law of gravitation first told us that every object in the universe was attracted by every other object. Einstein's theory also told us that attraction arose out of a space-time continuum. Einstein said that the attraction objects had for one another was actually their very reason for existence. The earth, the sun, and all the other celestial bodies would never have been formed if it weren't for the power of attraction.[5]

Even today, modern scientists still don't understand a lot of things about the power of attraction. Psychologists have studied these phenomena and have found them to be closely linked with the power of love but many aspects of these powers are still a mystery. With the help of Newton and Einstein, modern science has learned a lot but has still run up against a big problem in their understanding about attraction.

LIMITS OF SCIENTIFIC UNDERSTANDING

The problem about attraction, scientists say, is that the golden laws of Newton and Einstein only work well on our little old planet "Earth". The earlier theories that Newton and Einstein invented really don't explain the motion of the stars in their galaxies and the bending of light in our universe. In these vast galaxies, the laws that make sense on Earth really don't make sense in outer space. According to the laws of Newton and Einstein, it seems as though the stars should be thrown off in all directions! The whole universe shouldn't be functioning as well as it does and yet, something is holding it together. With this confusion in science, how do we explain the underlying order that has been maintained in our universe for billions of years?

One solution to the scientific problem of attraction was proposed by another scientist named Fritz Zwicky in 1933. Dr. Zwicky made a small step toward explaining attraction and the behavior of the stars when he proposed an 'unseen material' in the galaxies called 'dark matter'. Zwicky thought that dark matter would help to explain why the planets remained fixed in their orbits even when Newton and Einstein thought they should fly apart.[6] Dark matter has done a lot of things to help explain the behavior of the stars but it has still left a lot of questions unanswered. It often seems that science may never be able to explain this mysterious power known as attraction even as it continues on its quest for knowledge.

The most beautiful thing we can experience is
the mysterious. It is the source of all true art and all sci-
ence. He to whom this emotion is a stranger, who can no
longer pause to wonder and stand rapt in awe, is as
good as dead: his eyes are closed.7

— ALBERT EINSTEIN

The power of attraction is not only a great mystery in terms of the stars and planets but a great mystery in terms of people's lives. When two people come together, there is often an irresistible quality of attraction that overpowers every other desire they have. Because this power is so closely connected with the power of love, the attraction can even keep two people together forever. If we are able to understand the factors behind this amazing power that can keep two people together forever, we will have to look more deeply beyond science and reason. We will have to consult some of the great spiritual minds that can give us a deeper glance into the nature of both attraction and love.

ATTRACTION AND LOVE

The great spiritual teachers in history have always given us a solution to the problems that science and reason cannot seem to solve. Spiritual traditions have explained much more about the power of attraction by explaining to us more about a further power known as the power of love. This power that the spiritual teachers have spoken of is considered to be even stronger than the power of attraction because it has the potential to keep two people together for longer periods of time. When the simple power of attraction eventually fades, the power of love is there to sustain the relationship that otherwise would have ended.

In science, objects may first be attracted to each other by the simple fact that they are different and share qualities in each other that bring about a balance. Eventually, however, these same objects may be attracted by other objects and the initial bond that was formed can be broken. The power which keeps objects together and may actually hold the enormous galaxies together may be similar to what we call love in human relationships. It may be a lot more than just the simple power of attraction and may be something that science will never understand.

> Love is the motivating power of the universe...The majesty of this realization cannot be over-emphasized. We need to realize it far more deeply and potently than we do, for it constitutes the basic, fundamental character and quality of all events, no matter what the outer appearance may be.8
>
> — ALICE BAILEY

Love is far from being the kind of explanation that science is looking for in our modern world. Still, this refusal to look at the larger picture may actually be the reason that science often sees the questions as part of a 'dark matter'. What is needed is a wider vision of reality that is reflective on the totality of things. Love is not something which can control or manipulate nature. It serves no useful function in scientific thought. Love is a completely different kind of energy that is not as easy to explain and yet, it leads us toward a greater vision of wholeness and oneness in nature.

> *Reason deals only with particulars, whereas Love deals*
> *with entireties. This ability, often ascribed to intuition,*
> *is the capacity for instantaneous understanding with-*
> *out resorting to sequential symbol processing.*9
>
> — DR. DAVID R. HAWKINS

Science and reason are certainly impressive powers to be reckoned with but Love may also be something that has long since been unrecognized to the faint of heart. What many scientists have often recognized to be the power of attraction in individuals often goes unrecognized as the power of love.

LOVE AND SEPARATION

In order to understand love and the greater sense of wholeness that it helps us to achieve in our lives, it is important that we first contend with the idea of separation. Just like the concept of attraction, the concept of separation is also a much wider concept that can be applied to almost every aspect of our universe. People become separated in their marriages but the concept of separation extends even further than just human relationships. Separation is something that science teaches us when we are just in grade school. We learn that objects can be divided into two halves. "The universe is incredibly large," says the teacher "and we are incredibly small." In the beginning, science teaches us about a universe of great complexity and we learn about this with eager eyes.

We first learn that science is based on the necessary and useful idea of separation and yet, this very idea becomes something that is often a problem later in life. In order to cook our food, for instance, we need to know the scientific reason why the pots are separate from the pans. In order to serve the food, we need to know that the kitchen is separate from the dining room. Finally, in order to eat the meal, we need to know that the tables are separate from the chairs. This kind of knowledge is necessary for us to function and yet, it is not the kind of knowledge that really gives our lives meaning. It is not what gives our lives a lasting significance.

> *Learning, itself, like the classrooms in which it occurs, is temporary. The ability to learn has no value when change is no longer necessary. The eternally creative have nothing to learn.10*
>
> — A COURSE IN MIRACLES

Love is the thing that is found at the end of the road when all of our intricate concepts of separation and division will eventually leave us unfulfilled. Love rescues us from that split second with a completely different kind of perception. It comes to us directly and can even come in a single instant. In love, we have a larger vision of our dinner. We don't focus on the differences between the pots and the pans. We don't see just the tables and the chairs. Instead we have the impression of the entire house and our lovely mother as she makes us a delicious meal. In love, we eat the meal and feel grateful for all the things we have. We appreciate our family and the entire world around us.

> *Love can turn the cottage into a golden palace.11*
>
> — GERMAN PROVERB

Love seeks to unify rather than divide. It seeks to experience rather than observe. Love is a tendency toward a larger vision and does not focus so heavily on the ideas of division and separation. Instead, these ideas are subordinate to it and they merely serve as tools for love's larger purpose. This surprising conclusion was in fact obtained through a nationwide inquiry of some of America's most eminent mathematicians. The study was intended to discover the mathematician's working methods for discovering new truths and new formulas. One of these mathematicians included Albert Einstein and the conclusion that was made was the following:

Thinking plays only a subordinate part in the brief, decisive phase of the creative act itself.[12]

The missing link, which may help to explain many of the mysteries of science and eventually transform our entire way of looking at the world, may be love itself. It is only very recently that this connection between science and intuition is being understood in its wider significance.

Science has become extremely useful in its manner of dividing and separating objects into parts. It has produced many new materials that can be used for hundreds of billions of tasks and ideas. The pinnacle of modern science has even lead to the grand discoveries of quantum theory and non-linear dynamics. These systems go so far as to incorporate the scientists themselves into the picture of what is going on. They begin to unify the scientist with the science. They open up a whole new world beyond the initial division and separation that first seemed so fundamental.

The power of love goes even further to envision the

workings of the universe as a unified whole. This power may teach us that nobody's truth is any better than another's. It can even go so far as to present a vision of unconditional love which sees all things as equally important in the totality of the universe. This underlying vision of equality is one of the main principles that eventually turn the power of attraction into the power of love.

> *The secret of attraction is to love yourself. Attractive people judge neither themselves nor others. They are open to gestures of love. They think about love, and express their love in every action. They know that love is not a mere sentiment, but the ultimate truth at the heart of the universe.*[13]

— Deepak Chopra

Having come to a better understanding of the links between the power of attraction and the power of love, we can now go on to look at how attraction itself can grow to an even greater level of awareness into the awareness of love. The law of attraction can bring people to experience a larger vision than they had ever imagined and this is done through the power of our own thoughts. "We become what we think about" can be applied to larger and larger visions of the universe such that we can expand our own consciousness to greater and greater perspectives. The manner in which we do this is through an intimate understanding of the law of attraction.

– Part II –

The Law of
Attraction

*T*he spiritual law of attraction stated in another way says that, "Whatever we hold in mind tends to manifest in our lives." This is an interpretation given to us from Dr. David R. Hawkins in many of his lectures and speeches around the world. It has also been expressed by Napoleon Hill. In general, it simply means that we tend to attract the things that we think about or focus on in our lives. By instilling our emotional energy into certain things, we call them toward us each day.

> *Our minds become magnetized with the dominating thoughts we hold in our minds and these magnets attract to us the forces, the people, the circumstances of life which harmonize with the nature of our dominating thoughts.*[4]
>
> — NAPOLEON HILL

Keeping a positive attitude certainly isn't an easy thing to do. Each day, people will tell themselves many negative things. These negative ideas will sometimes be expressed in the light of day by a seemingly happy person and yet, when we get to know the people who are thinking these ideas, we may find that they are actually quite depressed and afraid of many things. People make a lot of decisions based on these negative feelings and it isn't always apparent how much it is affecting their lives. It will often appear to be quite bad when you take a closer look inside.

The negative tendencies that people pursue in their lives often help to confirm the initial fears that they have. They lose their jobs, their friends and their closest loved ones to problems that seem beyond their control. This seems impossible to change and yet, the law of attraction tells us something different. People's thoughts and decisions often promote the very kind of negative evidence that they initially set out to prove. They are the very cause of their own problems! The negative ideas that people project often function in a similar manner as a "self-fulfilling prophecy". By focusing on the negative, the negative comes to pass. The law of attraction tells us that, whatever we give our attention to becomes our point of attraction. It becomes the thing that we magnetize into our lives. This is even true for the things we try to separate ourselves from or fight against because we find that we are still giving these "negative" things our constant attention.

Let's look at an example. Someone decides that the worst thing in the world would be for their loved one to leave them. They worry about this day and night. It is their worst fear and they can't get it out of their mind. As they focus on this fear, they find that they simply cannot trust the person they are with. They are constantly second guessing this person and accusing them of the fears they hold inside. Instead of showing them love and affection, they are actually driving this person away.

When we create something, we always create it first in a thought form. If we are basically positive in attitude, expecting and envisioning pleasure, satisfaction and happiness, we will attract and create people, situations, and events which conform to our positive expectations.[15]

— SHAKTI GAWAIN

Getting over our fears and negative emotions can be quite a challenge when we are applying the law of attraction in our lives. In order to be successful and attract what is positive, it is helpful to see the challenges ahead. If we know what to expect in terms of the law of attraction, we will be prepared to attract only the things that are truly best for us in our lives. In this way, we will avoid the fears and confusions and find the love and understanding along the way.

OPPOSITES SEEM TO ATTRACT

You've heard this said a million times and it certainly seems to be true in many cases. Opposites seem to attract. Oftentimes, couples seem as though they were two very different people. One is active, one is passive. One is cool and one is hot. Although these differences seem to exist on the surface, couples that stay together also have something more and this underlying vibration is the real thing that makes the attraction so powerful. People seem to be attracted to the qualities in another person that make them different. This is the way it appears on the surface and yet, this isn't the truth. As time goes on, the differences that seemed to attract these people no longer have the initial appeal that they first had.

Couples who are mainly focused on the differences that we have with each other, tend to argue and even despise those same qualities that seemed so great in the beginning. They often find that they have nothing in common after they have been together for a little while. In this case, they may start to realize that they need some similarities in order to balance things out.

Yin and yang tend to attract each other to create a balance but it is the underlying "balance" or "wholeness" that is really so attractive to these individuals. It is not the qualities of yin or yang themselves. An underlying vibration is necessary in order to keep those opposites together. The essential quality that is necessary to keep people together is often thought to be this wider vision of 'love' or 'peace'. Without this underlying power, the universe and the relationship would fly apart just like both Newton and Einstein might have helped us predict.

Although it may be true that opposites seem to attract, it is an even greater truth that opposites are only kept together by an underlying vibration of love. This power of love is an even greater power of attraction that supersedes the powers of yin and yang and becomes, for many people, the supreme power of attraction in the universe.

THE VOID

Another challenging idea along the path to creating our own destiny involves the idea of the void. This is an idea which originates in the idea of separation and can be seen as a way of looking at life or at the universe. In simple terms, the void can best be understood in terms of the things that we WANT and the things that we DON'T WANT. If there is a thing that we DON'T WANT, we focus on it wherever we go and divide up our experiences in relation to this hidden idea of emptiness or "negation".

The "void" is an idea that has been presented to many spiritual seekers along their path and this is actually a form of negative thinking that is very subtle and insidious to the advanced seeker. We all give power to our hidden negativities and they take on a larger and larger context as we develop. This context, when it reaches its widest conception, is something that eventually manifests as the "void". If we can look more closely at this idea and try to uncover the negativity in our own thinking, it may help us to open it into a wider context of awareness. This wider context would, by its very nature, be a more attractive context simply because of the larger awareness that it allows.

First, let's look at an example. Some people are always dreading the future. They imagine that they will eventually have problems with their health or with their finances. They are always worried about what will happen to them down the road. After worrying about these outcomes, they find that they are very tired and need to take a break from the draining problems in their life. They decide to take a break from work because they are beginning to feel sick. They may stay home or even decide to quit their jobs because they "just can't take it anymore". "I hate my job" is one of the most common ideas that people tell themselves. "My relationships never work" is another common negation. With this kind of thinking, the future always seems to arrive with extreme predictability.

Inevitably, negative people tend to be viewed by others as lazy or irresponsible. People don't want a negative person working at their company or hanging around their circle of friends. These people often lose their jobs and find themselves incapable of paying their bills after their relationships go sour. They are often abandoned by their mates and can even enter into a severe form of depression. Oftentimes, they will even develop health problems and find that all of their original predictions about the doom and gloom of the world have come true.

Whoso diggeth a pit shall fall therein.[16]

— PROVERBS

People who see a negative future become discontented. This seems obvious and yet, negative people seem intensely committed to their own negativity. It is as though they felt there was some great honor in seeing the bad side of things. The evidence they were looking for about the world and the negative "reality" of life always seems to arrive with predictable accuracy because the law of attraction is working in all areas of the universe. In order to stop this negative thinking, it is best to look at the way it manifests itself so as to uncover a larger field of attraction and open ourselves to more positive energies.

RUNNING FROM FEAR

If we decide to focus on fear and grief, we will surely attract these kinds of things into our life and feel a certain perverted satisfaction that our vision of negativity was initially correct. Even when we run from these fears, we cannot escape them. Running from fear only instills the energy into our lives and helps it to manifest as a reality. Running from fear is not the way to alleviate this negative emotion. In fact, battling with any kind of negative emotion is only another way of attracting it into our lives.

If you have ever seen a person who is suffering from a mental illness, they can often be seen muttering to themselves or carrying on in a very strange manner. They may have acquired a sickness that paralyzes them in their lives. They will engage others with senseless arguments in order to satisfy their own sense of frustration or grief. What is so

interesting is that others, who are less disturbed, will sometimes engage these people in elaborate discussions possibly
in the hope of curing them or changing their minds. Quite
often, the efforts are fruitless and only make the sane person
appear worse off than when they began.

When a sick person and a well person get together, it is
more likely that the two will both end up sick rather than the
two of them both becoming well. Engaging in a battle over
negative ideas is likely to only produce more negative ideas
so that nothing is solved. This same idea holds true when it
comes to fear. Engaging our fear as though it were something we should be afraid of is not the correct course.
Instead of running from the things we fear or fighting
against the things we dislike, we might choose instead not to
waste our energy. We might take the high road instead and
choose not to give in to the secret attraction that these arguments may have. We might turn the other cheek and look for
something more positive to pursue.

Running from fear is only a way of expressing our own
belief in the very power of fear. FDR's famous quote "We
have nothing to fear but fear itself" profoundly suggests that
fear is an empty idea with no power in and of itself. As long
as we don't feed these fears, they will have nothing to live
on and will eventually dissolve in the light of our own
awareness. The law of attraction teaches us that this kind of
positive thinking will only build on itself as we apply it in
our lives. We begin to find that our courage is growing at
enormous rates each day and the things we thought we
should fear were only figments of our own imagination.

ACCEPTING OUR GRIEF

Depression is a similar energy as fear but it is also a very common and natural phase of a person's development. As we learn to incorporate the negative ideas that we encounter in life, we also learn to reach for a larger context in which to understand these negative emotions. This larger context may eventually lead to a healthier attitude but this certainly doesn't happen overnight. As we begin to identify our negative emotions, fear and grief will begin to dissolve. The outside will eventually conform to our inner vision of things as we put the law of attraction into action.

It takes a lot of practice to overcome sadness and grief in our everyday lives and sometimes these emotions can go on for years. Oftentimes, people will turn to anti-depressant medication as a way of helping them get over these negative emotions. Anti-depressants can be very helpful in learning how to turn away from negative ideas and emotions and to incorporate more positive habits into our lives. Experiencing grief or depression can be seen as a positive step toward spiritual growth even if we need to turn to some help from science and medicine. We eventually discover that we were the inventors of those fears and that there wasn't any realistic basis for them in the first place. Looking at our own depression and sadness is a necessary phase of development and can be viewed in a positive light if we allow ourselves the chance to grow. The true reality in the universe is love but coming to this awareness is often a very long and arduous process. Eventually, we find the strength to view our grief as a temporary illusion that can also be dissolved in the light of consciousness.

The opposite of love is fear, but what is
all-encompassing can have no opposite.[7]

— A COURSE IN MIRACLES

Many of our negative impressions come from an under-lying belief that everything is useless, empty and essentially a large void. People often talk about a sense of emptiness in their lives and a void in their hearts that simply cannot be filled no matter what they do. If this void were truly the ulti-mate reality of the universe, then there would certainly be a good reason to assume that everything was ultimately nega-tive. This, however, is simply not the case as both science and spirituality have come to show us. The one simple understanding that someone can have about "nothingness" is that, by its own very definition it is "Not".

POSITIVE REFLECTIONS ON THE VOID

According to the great masters and many of the more modern interpretations of science, anything that can be per-ceived or thought of is always considered to be subjective in some sense. This is why the law of attraction works so well in our lives. Ideas about "nothingness" or the "void" do not have any real existence apart from a person's subjective experience. We are the ultimate creators of our own reality and coming to this realization is the only thing we need to do before our own happiness can become a priority. We eventually learn that there could never be a "void" if there were not someone like us to experience it in the first place. The observer, our Self, is the subjective reality which becomes the very proof that the "void" does not exist. We become our own proof about the reality of the world around us. This has been the natural progression of many great mystics over time, many of whom have experienced deep periods of depression or what is often called 'The Dark Night of the Soul' before they have reached Enlightenment. Eckhart Tolle has expressed this idea about his own fear and the idea of the "void" in his book The Power of Now.

> *I could feel myself being sucked into a void. It felt as though the void was inside myself rather than outside. Suddenly, there was no more fear, and I let myself fall into that void. I have no recollection of what happened after that. I was awakened by the chirping of a bird outside the window. I had never heard such a sound before.....Tears came into my eyes.....I recognized the room, and yet I knew that I had never truly seen it before...For the next five months, I lived in a state of uninterrupted deep peace and bliss.*[18]

Eckhart Tolle's experience of the "void" was an extremely profound experience and one that he seemed to attract into his life before he found the ability to overcome it and thereby let it go. After his experience, it is plain to see that another focus took over his attention and the negative ideas were seen as truly non-existent. Tolle could not recollect anything from his experience of the void because such an experience is actually non-existent in ultimate reality. He went on to have many subsequent experiences which had a positive quality because he let go of his false conception of the void. Theodore Nottingham has also expressed a similar idea about negative emotions in his reference to the teachings of Peter Ouspensky.

The purpose of dealing with negative emotions
is to a) clean up our inner life so that b) we can
use the energies precisely for experiences
of higher consciousness.[19]

— PETER OUSPENSKY

After working on our negative emotions for so long, a saturation point is eventually reached and a new realization crystallizes in our minds. In terms of the grand lesson that many spiritual teachers have tried to impart to us, Dr. David R. Hawkins' published works are widely recognized as evidence of a very advanced state of spiritual awareness such as the one being discussed here. Dr. Hawkins has also spoken extensively on the idea of the "void" and has given valuable insights into the interpretation of this idea about "nothingness" in spiritual experience.

Void is a state created solely by the mind's belief
in it as an actual possibility. The only actual
possibilities in Reality are Is-ness, Allness and
Beingness. It is obvious that theoretical opposites
to these would then be conceived.[20]

— HAWKINS

Although theoretical opposites to what "Is" are often conceived, these opposites are only temporary diversions from the truth. They are not accurate pictures of reality. Dr. Hawkins explains that concepts such as "off" when used to designate the condition of a light switch, do not actually refer to a separate state. "Off" is merely a convenient idea that we use to designate what would more accurately be referred to as "not on".

Although this sounds like an insignificant point, Dr. Hawkins explains that it is actually very significant to our underlying perceptions about the world around us. We keep imagining that there are objective realities to the negative ideas we possess. Dr. Hawkins stresses the importance of understanding that there is never an actual state of "offness" in an electrical circuit but only the presence of *electricity* or the absence of *electricity*.[21] The problems that we experience between love and separation always stem from a misconception that there are certain states in our lives where there is "lack" or "emptiness". Lack or emptiness, however, is simply not a reality that holds any true existence beyond our own perception of it.

Without realizing what we are doing, we attract certain ideas into our lives. Oftentimes we cannot see this because we don't see the immense power that our minds possess. We find later that we are very depressed and experiencing a sense of emptiness in our lives but we don't know why. Many spiritual practices attempt to get us to a place where we are feeling good more of the time. If we can eliminate our negative tendencies, then we tend to attract more positive things that improve our feelings. Ideas, in general, tend to be magnetic. They attract more of the same and we see a momentum that eventually starts to go in the right direction. By gently guiding our thoughts and our feelings to a better place, we become more adept at this practice. We learn to take a nice walk when we are feeling bad or spend some time in appreciation of nature. We learn meditation and how to guide our thoughts and emotions into a more harmonious stream and the good events will only follow once we learn to change our minds. In a universe that is based upon the law of attraction, what could be more important than our own good feelings?

ATTRACTOR FIELDS

Although love is considered to be a power even greater than reason, science itself has certainly come a long way in explaining the power of attraction. Modern medicine can do wondrous things to help us along to a better vision of reality and help to boost us out of the negative thinking that we originally had entrained ourselves into. The tendency of more and more people to reach a more holistic vision of reality is getting closer and closer everyday. The progress of science has continued in recent decades with the advancement of non-linear dynamics and, what is known as, "Chaos theory" in science. Despite its inherent challenges, science has continued to press on and to champion more and more elaborate explanations about the power of attraction. In recent years, the new science of nonlinear dynamics has posed the idea of 'strange attractors' which help to explain more about our objects' behavior in the universe.

> *'Attractor field' is a term derived from nonlinear dynamics and signifies that within what appears to be random or unconnected occurrences, there is actually an invisible, organizing pattern field of influence that affects the occurrence of phenomena within each level of consciousness.*[22]

> — HAWKINS

Scientists now believe that the universe may be just a large conglomeration of attractor patterns under which all of nature is guided. These attractor patterns might be viewed as the underlying cause or 'Mind' of the universe with which science is learning more and more everyday. In this sense,

PART II. THE LAW OF ATTRACTION

the decision making process may be part of a much larger and more essential pattern of attraction that we are only just beginning to understand in our modern conception of scientific understanding.

> *The decision making process is a function of consciousness itself; the mind makes choices based on millions of pieces of data and their correlations and projections, far beyond conscious comprehension, and with enormous rapidity. This is a global function dominated by energy patterns that the new science of nonlinear dynamics terms 'attractors'.*[23]

— HAWKINS

Dr. David R. Hawkins is a leading scientist and lecturer on the topic of both science and spirituality. He has introduced the idea that the underlying cause of people's behavior, and of the activities in nature, are actually guided by these larger 'attractor fields' which are thought of as 'fields of consciousness'. These different fields organize the behavior of objects in nature and tend to attract things into their field according to a greater degree of order that they inspire. Although he is not an advocate of any particular field in general, one of the larger attractor fields that Dr. Hawkins has spoken of is the field of Taoism or "The Tao".

TAOISM

Taoism is a great spiritual tradition which is based on the teachings of Lao-tzu. The Tao, in the broadest sense, is the way the universe functions, the path taken by natural events. It is characterized by spontaneous creativity and by the regular

www.guideforliving.com   27

changes of phenomena. Through the techniques and practices of Taoism, many dedicated followers have claimed to achieve a greater harmony in their lives and a wider expansion of consciousness. For them, the incoherent has become coherent and they have finally experienced a grand vision of peace and order in their lives.

To the mind that is still, the whole universe surrenders.[24]

— LAO-TZU

Taoism teaches that, in nature, spring follows from winter and day follows from night. These cycles, that we also learn about in our science classes, proceed without effort. The Tao has always been considered to be the way of the universe; the norm, the rhythm, and the guiding power behind nature. It is important to recognize, however, that the Tao is spirit, not matter. It is an inexhaustible energy that flows stronger the more it is drawn upon. It is an energy which is very similar to the energy of Love.

Love focuses on giving to others and transforming rather than controlling. If the power underlying all of nature were similar to the Power of Love, then Lao-Tzu would have been right even long before the scientists had begun theorizing about the workings of the stars.

The reason why the universe is eternal is that it does not live for itself; it gives life to others as it transforms.[25]

— LAO-TZU

The goal of Taoists is to attain harmony with the Tao. This attainment of harmony with the Tao is also seen as living in accord with nature. Nature is something that should not be exploited and abused, it should be befriended and appreciated. The ideal man in Taoism is one who, through the naturalness of his existence, becomes self-sufficient and not dependent upon wealth or social realms. In this way, true happiness can be found.

The yin-yang doctrine is based on the concept that there are continuous transformations within the Tao. The principle that embraces nature is divided into two opposites or principles that oppose one another. The principles of yang are light, heat, Heaven, male and sun. The principles of the yin are darkness, cool, earth, female and moon. Everything consists of this balance. The production of yin from yang and yang from yin occurs in a cyclical motion. It is continuous and it happens in such as way so that no principle ever dominates the other. Yin and Yang express the contrasting aspects and interrelationships of everything in the universe.

For a Taoist, the objective is to reach and maintain harmony with the Tao. When this harmony is reached enlightenment has been achieved. In Enlightenment, we accept the plainness of our life. The truths of the Tao cannot be found in any doctrine. Instead, they are found when a person's energy is balanced and their mind is clear. Taoism promotes simplicity, openness, and wisdom. Once you have realized it, you have openness to life, a tranquility of mind and a reserved genius. The Taoist sage is not arrogant and does not discriminate between opposites. They are indifferent to worldly affairs and are at peace.

In such loving attraction live earth and sky: As when blessed rain falls soft upon the earth, Mankind and

*Nature could unite like lovers — Free of law, free of
command, People would finally be at peace.*[26]

— Lao-Tzu

As we develop our understanding of the Tao, we learn to
incorporate its ideas into our own lives and to experience a
more profound sense of harmony all around us. Things start
to work much better in our lives and there seems to be a lot
less problems to contend with. The power of both attraction
and love are working in our life to bring us to a greater sense
of wholeness and unity each day.

Although we are constantly attracted by the experiences
that these higher fields of consciousness can bring, we also
find that our old habits tend to return to us and are always
pulling us back down into the more narrow energy fields
that we initially experienced in our lives. These lower fields
of energy still exist in other people and other places. We
only learn to change our lifestyles by aligning ourselves
with the wider attractor fields of both love and peace.

Commitment

Choosing a direction is the first step in aligning ourselves with wider attractor fields. Commitment is the element of attraction that makes the journey a likely success
because things start to take on a quality of permanence. This
is obvious in human relationships but not as commonly
understood in terms of spiritual pursuits. Commitment can
keep a marriage together but can also make a spiritual journey a grand success.

Until one is committed there is hesitating, the chance to draw back, always ineffectiveness. Concerning all acts of initiative (and creation), there is one elementary truth, the ignorance of which kills countless ideas and splendid plans. That the moment one definitely commits oneself, Providence moves, too. All sorts of things occur to help one that would never otherwise have occurred. A whole stream of events issues from the decision, raising in one's favor all manner of unforeseen incidents and meetings and material assistance which no man could have dreamed would have come his way.[27]

— Johan Wolfgang von Goethe

Goethe knew that nothing can come about until there is commitment. This is true because the law of attraction will only allow us to have the things we think about each day. Until we are committed to placing our energy in one certain area, the success of our endeavors cannot be realized. Goethe also expressed this sentiment in relation to the power of love when he said, "We are shaped and fashioned by what we love." It would seem from his ideas that we are not only affected by the things we focus on in our minds, but especially by the things we love.

– Part III –

Career

*O*nce we begin to recognize that our old way of seeing things is attracting negative things into our lives, we begin to feel the attraction to become something else. We begin to focus on the things we love and this takes place in greater and greater intensity as we adopt a wider view of the world around us. We learn to accept things and to even experience gratitude for the way things are because this brings more joy and happiness to us. It is a difficult task at first as our old ways of seeing the world tend to permeate every area of our lives and negativity has become a very bad habit. It is even hard, in the beginning, to root out our negative emotions as their source tends to be very cunning and hidden from our view. In our work and at home we can especially see that we have established many bad habits that keep us stuck in the more narrow fields of consciousness and the magnetic power of these old ways is very hard to overcome.

The difficulty of inner work results from the great
effort required to escape from the familiar gravity
of lower attractor fields and move to the influence
of a higher field.[28]

— HAWKINS

In order to arrive at this higher level of consciousness, we eventually find that we must begin to apply a new awareness to every aspect of our lives. The spiritual effort becomes a daily practice that we apply to our careers and our relationships. At first the efforts seem very difficult but eventually we come to see that something else has been working in our lives which is far beyond our own personal power and has begun helping us along the way. In fact, this power has been there all along but we were not aware of its presence until now.

Our careers require extreme amounts of time and effort in our lives and yet, this area is often relegated to the 'back burner' when we think about spirituality. We think of our spiritual lives as a time to read or meditate and our careers as a time to make money and survive. Nothing could be further from the truth. Our careers are an intricate element of our spiritual lives and an area that needs considerable attention if we are going to attract positive energy into our lives. We will have to learn to think more positively about our careers if we are going to attract positive energy throughout our entire day.

A career involves more than just a job. A career involves a progression or an increase that brings us toward a greater level of success in our job. This happens by becoming more advanced in our spiritual pursuits. It is often a surprise to many people who practice spirituality that some of the most successful career minded individuals are also some of the most spiritual people in the world. It is the underlying drive to succeed that fuels people's desire to have a career and facing the daily challenges of a career is a great way to improve ourselves.

DESTRUCTIVE THINKING

Many people are dead set against money and careers. A common sentiment is that "money is the root of all evil" and many Americans believe that the corporations and the government are only out to exploit people for power and control. Money is often set in a bad light by those of us who may study spirituality or religion. The Eastern traditions often emphasize the importance of being "unattached" to wealth and success so that many people misunderstand the intentions of corporations or millionaires who are in possession of great wealth. Having a lot of money does not necessarily mean that there is going to be an attachment to money. Indeed, the Biblical quote alluded to above actually reads "The **love** of money is the root of all evil."[29] (1 Timothy 6: 10, my emphasis) Many great millionaires become philanthropists and help to solve enormous problems all over the world. It is the attitude that we carry toward wealth and power that creates the attachment that many religions often speak of. This is an idea which is very often misunderstood and which often leads to destructive thinking.

This misconception about the meaning of "attachment" often leads many people to think that you have to be poor and unemployed in order to be spiritual. A reverse sort of egotism can even set up with this kind of thinking where people will oftentimes see themselves to be 'better' than the rich and successful simply because they don't have any money or success themselves. As time goes on, these less fortunate people become unhappy in their lives because the rewards they imagined themselves to eventually gain for their commitment to poverty were somehow not materializing in the way they had hoped. They become angry at the world as if some mysterious enemy had taken over their lives and made them fall into a terrible misfortune. This problem only comes about as a result of people's negative thinking. They imagine a future when everything will fall apart for the rich and successful and they will get their just rewards. The future never arrives for having lived a life of poverty and unemployment and they wonder "What went wrong?"

The attachments of the ego take place in all areas of the world and not just for the rich and successful minded people. A career can certainly become a place where people abuse their powers and exploit the less fortunate people of the world but it is also a place where the less fortunate can become bitter and resentful. The world around them simply becomes dark and hopeless because they never made the effort to overcome their unfortunate state. They hate the people in power and resent the larger order that has come to exist around them. Overcoming this kind of negative thinking is extremely hard. We have to start to consider the possibility that powerful people may only be doing their best to make the world a better place. We may not understand who the corrupt people are and who the philanthropists are until we have walked a mile in their shoes. A better place to focus our energies would be in our own lives and on our own negative thinking. In this way, we may learn to overcome these destructive thoughts and lead ourselves out of the negative patterns we have set up in our lives.

Constructive Thinking

A career is the perfect place to set up your spiritual workshop because it is an area that requires a great deal of time and energy everyday and involves almost every aspect of spiritual principles in order that you make it successful. Even if you are starting out at the very bottom as a dishwasher in a hot and dirty kitchen, you can make your career into an intensely spiritual pursuit that will eventually lead to other jobs and a more productive career that brings happiness and joy. Everyone needs a job of some kind in order to feel productive and the simplest or the most complex jobs are equally fertile ground for spiritual practices.

The key to long term success is not in the particular job that you are doing. The key is in working on yourself as you do your particular job. This is constructive thinking because it makes it possible to use your time even more productively. When there is not an extremely important task immediately at hand, you can focus your mind on the present moment and simply experience your own inner consciousness. This effort will eventually widen the attractor field in which you find yourself and open up greater amounts of energy into your life. If you make sure and work harder on yourself than you do on your particular job, success will surely follow wherever you go. Once you begin dedicating hours a day to your personal development, your success will not be far behind.

THE DETAILS OF LIFE

Oftentimes, spiritual enthusiasts may tend to think that it is 'ok' to avoid the details of life because spirituality is associated with keeping things 'simple'. We think we should live simple lives and we can ignore the details. We don't worry about mortgages or going to the dentist or sorting through the mail. We like to wear sandals and meditate. We like to feed the pigeons and sit on a park bench. Keeping life simple is certainly an essential spiritual principle but paying attention to the details of life is also something that we shouldn't be afraid of. Looking at the details doesn't have to mean looking at the details of 'worry' and 'fear'. The details can in fact be extremely beautiful.

Here are a few details that we certainly don't have to

worry about and that don't help us to move forward in our lives. First of all, we don't have to worry about the detail of "urgency". Urgency suggests that things aren't exactly as they need to be and therefore the universe has somehow been created 'wrong'. This is a negative idea that only feeds the flames of our discontent. We don't have to worry about the detail of "being in a hurry" because we now feel confident that everything is happening for a reason. Similarly, we don't have to worry about the detail of "recognition" or the detail of "popularity" when we go about making a career for ourselves. If we have faith in the larger attractor fields, we know that our just rewards will eventually come to us after we have taken care of the more important issues at hand. Finally, we don't have to worry about the detail of "tomorrow" and this idea is very eloquently expressed in the first book of the New Testament.

> *Can any of you by worrying add a single hour to the span of your life? ... So do not worry about tomorrow, for tomorrow will bring worries of its own. Today's trouble is enough for today.*[30]
>
> —MATT. 6:27, 34

Details that consume us never help to accomplish anything worthwhile in the end and it is easy to overlook the important details when we are running around like a chicken with our heads cut off. We may simply be trying too hard to control the wrong things and so the more important details tend to elude us. Eventually we have no energy left for the most important things which are the experience of joy and happiness in our lives.

Once we've learned to look for spiritual truth, we will begin to find it in every area of our lives. This will especially be true in terms of the details. The details of a beautiful flower will be seen in the same way as the details of the pile of mail at the front door. Even a can of garbage can be seen as beautiful, as Dr. Hawkins notably states:

> One adds the pathway of the heart by making a decision to be unconditionally loving to all that is encountered..... This means one has to learn to love even a garbage can. When seen correctly, garbage cans are not only loveable but beautiful and perfect......
> When the beauty and loveableness of the beat-up old garbage can reveals itself, the spiritual seeker can affirm that they are well along the way.[31]
>
> — HAWKINS

After we have calmed down and begun to attract more positive energies into our lives, all the details of life become stunningly beautiful and full of promise. We can return to the details about the mortgage and the dentist which at first seemed so fraught with worry and fear. We may begin to see great opportunities in the pile of mail instead of endless problems and worries in each bill. The details of life provide us with a great opportunity to experience beauty and joy but only if we approach them with the right attitude. If we carry an attitude of worry and fear, the details will also express this back to us as objects of worry and fear. If we carry an attitude of joy and gratitude, the details of life will express these more positive ideas instead.

Little jobs can also be a joy if we learn to practice a spiritual presence in our lives. A wider success will eventually come from what first seemed like an unimportant detail in life and success will become the rule instead of the exception.

> *Don't be afraid to give your best to what seemingly are small jobs. Every time you conquer one it makes you that much stronger. If you do the little jobs well, the big ones tend to take care of themselves.*[32]

> — DALE CARNEGIE

Letting the big jobs take care of themselves is a profound idea but something that should not be misunderstood in terms of being 'lazy' or apathetic. We don't ignore the importance of the big jobs when we take on the attention to the smaller ones. It simply becomes the case that we understand we aren't in control of the big jobs. We control only the little things and keep the big jobs at the forefront of our awareness. By staying aware of what is ultimately most important, we actually call this into our lives according to the law of attraction.

One of the greatest examples of this kind of behavior can be seen in the activity of thousands of individual ants. Each of them has one small job to do but they also have a larger pattern in mind as they work together to create an elaborate ant colony. Underneath the seemingly small attention to detail that each ant displays, is the larger vision of the colony. The queen ant is often seen as the 'leader' and yet she never gives any direct orders to the ants. The queen doesn't "tell" the ants what to do. Each ant reacts to its own individual scent and leaves its own chemical trail which provides a stimulus to the other ants. This is the law of attraction working in each ant's life. Genetics and other factors certainly play a role in the "decisions" of each ant but there is still an autonomous presence in each ant so that they can make their own decisions within the larger framework.

Despite the lack of a central "leader", ant colonies still have an amazingly complex pattern of behavior and individual ants have even been shown to be capable of solving complex geometric problems. An example of this is the fact that ants commonly determine the furthest distance from each of the entrances to their hills in order to know where the best place to dispose of their dead. The ants individually measure the distance between hills in order to locate the grave sites for other ants. This is a higher order of consciousness at work and something that reflects the greater good of each member of the colony.

This larger vision of order and harmony that can be seen in the behavior of ants and many other groups of animals, is a necessary element behind the energy which contributes to the completion of even the smallest jobs in our world. The larger spiritual energy fields are acted on through the individual attention to the smaller details in life. These more detailed jobs become the active purpose of our daily experience through their connection to the larger purpose. The larger vision fuels the smaller attention to detail and each of us can then move along to a greater and greater awareness of what is.

EMERGENCE IN CAREER

In science, the concept of 'emergence' can be used to describe the way small jobs are ultimately related to their larger attractor fields. This concept of emergence helps to explain how these smaller, simpler tasks receive a spiritual energy through their connection to the larger whole. This is the idea that more complex patterns arise from the more simple details of our behavior.

For an activity to be thought of as 'emergent' it is generally seen as unpredictable from a lower level. To the casual observer, it may appear as though the person is simply doing a very menial task that is unimportant. It is unpredictable and unprecedented, however, when the reasons for this simple behavior beome more apparent in terms of a larger scheme. Although they cannot be explained by reference to typical explanations, a more complex explanation helps them to make sense.[33]

In a typical job, a common reason for taking that job may be 'money' or 'opportunity for promotion'. These are common ideas that serve as simple reasons for going to work. They are fairly simplistic but are still commonly held to be the driving force behind many people's careers. If a person is doing the job in order to increase their spiritual connection, however, this may represent a new level in the system's evolution. This would be an example of an emergent pattern that could not be readily observable from simply looking at the individual person. It is a pattern that gives a greater significance to the person's job and would ultimately become more apparent as time went on because the persons career would begin to visibly reflect this hidden dimension. As the person's career progressed, the emergent pattern would be an extremely helpful and productive pattern of activity that could be seen more as a property of the collective whole rather than just a simple financial pattern.

In many cases, a person's behavior in their job cannot be

explained according to lower level reasoning. Many physical properties in nature are the same such as that of molecules which transmit sound. There aren't any specific qualities in the molecules which explain the larger pattern of behavior such as the transmission of sound. Emergent structures are patterns seen from a single event or a simple rule and yet they are still inherent in each individual part of the system. Although there is nothing that is immediately evident as an explanation for the behavior, the interactions of each part in relation to the larger whole lead to an order and harmony that can be seen by each person.

MONEY

Money is one of the most common explanations that people use to describe the reasoning behind their job. It is an extremely simple explanation and yet it is often considered less than adequate to bring complete happiness in their lives. "I've got to pay the bills" is a simple yet insufficient reason for obtaining joy and harmony in our work. If we are to experience real happiness and a strong purpose in our jobs, we must typically involve ourselves more intimately with our job performance and make some kind of alternate contribution either to the larger purpose of the company or to ourselves. Money plays an important part in this sense but other factors such as improving our quality of life also plays a role.

Successful people make money. It's not that people who make money become successful, but that successful people attract money. They bring success to what they do.[34]

— WAYNE DYER

Donald Trump has expressed the importance of money in terms of "a scorecard that tells me I've won and by how much". Trump is one of the most successful real estate developers of the modern age. He is more associated with wealth and money than even Bill Gates, who is the richest man in the world. Donald Trump has explained that his happiness really doesn't come from the money but from the business dealings themselves. Trump obtains his joy in 'making the deal' and this only happens to generate large amounts of money as a byproduct. He certainly pays attention to the money but the real joy is located in the 'deal'. If Donald Trump couldn't make deals, he simply wouldn't be happy.[35]

The pattern that emerges in the career of Donald Trump is one of many successful 'deal makers'. At first glance, people see the money as the motivating factor because it is the simplest and most easy explanation. Of course, the money scorecard is definitely important but it isn't the whole picture. When we look closer, we see a more complex pattern emerging.

In other fields, money may also have a certain ability to serve as a scorecard but this scorecard may become less useful as we move into more subjective fields of work. Art, for example, is not always judged so well through its monetary value and yet, it can still be a very good way to make some initial judgments. In terms of money and our careers, we will always have to take into consideration the importance of this simple explanation but this is only an initial way of seeing the larger pattern in a career. As we begin to focus our spiritual efforts in our job and career, a larger pattern may eventually emerge which can bring even greater success.

GOAL SETTING

One of the most important elements to having a successful career is to think big. The more you are able to put into your mind, the better things you are going to achieve. Earl Nightengale has also said that a person's common problem is not that they can't achieve their goal, but that they never set the proper goals that they need to be successful. Setting the right goals is a very big part of achievement itself. A goal is sort of like having a dream that includes a specific deadline. The more detailed the goal is, the better. "Having a million dollars" is a great goal but it isn't a very detailed one. A goal needs to explain the useful aspects that are going to assist you in your achievement.[36]

Daily habits are a great way to fill out the details of a realistic goal. We have to make sure our work ethic will match with our dreams and ask ourselves if we are dedicated enough to carry through with the effort. The financial rewards are only one small part of a realistic goal. They will not typically work as a sole motivator in our career. Attention to spiritual values in our careers can bring about a more comprehensive practice which can then return to us as a worthy investment in the future. We will eventually learn to function in a productive way with the other people in our lives who will help to make us more successful as we move along our career path.

– PART IV –

RELATIONSHIPS

*R*elationships are often what inspire us each morning to get out of bed and make an effort to improve our lives. The power of attraction is never more obvious than in the case of two people in love. This power makes each of us more eager and willing to make that extra effort in our lives and to go on with each successive day. The power in a relationship is also the thing which fuels people's sense of spiritual effort in their lives and gives them a sense of gratitude for their life.

ROMANCE

Romance is one of the most powerful energies that inspire an interest in the spiritual life. It is the romantic ideal that is so intimately tied to our experience of love and ultimately to the greater meaning behind life.

> — *how fortunate are you and I, whose home is*
> *timelessness: we who have wandered down from*
> *fragrant mountains of eternal now to frolic in such*
> *mysteries as birth and death a day(or maybe even less)*[27]
>
> — E.E. CUMMINGS

Some of the most romantic ideas have been expressed to us through art and poetry and these fields are especially disposed to inspire a greater vision of what is sacred and most important to us in our lives. Romance is also closely associated with love as it helps to express the challenges that are encountered when two people strive to have a loving relationship. Love is always fraught with challenges and romance helps us to express these challenges in a more positive light.

One of the more widely held beliefs about romantic love is that there is often a mere 'randomness' to the encounter which eventually can be seen to have a wider significance in the more meaningful pattern of love. Romantic love is also commonly thought to involve an overcoming of obstacles in which the larger pattern is somehow threatened by a less meaningful element. Romantic love cannot be controlled and is therefore thought to be something beyond the individuals themselves.

The pattern of romantic love initially emerged in the Middle Ages when it was often the case that insurmountable barriers would separate two would-be lovers from their true destiny of eternal union. This is the typical image that we have when we think of romantic visions. The overcoming of age-old barriers often results in a strong regard for 'winning the love' of the other person and it has motivated great efforts to be expressed through poetry, songs and heroic battles since the earliest ages. Even today, writers go to great efforts to express this ongoing struggle and to revive the old passions of the earlier romantic ideal. We strive to express these ideas in the same way that we always have because the themes are always the same and will never change.

We think, sometimes, there's not a dragon left.
Not one brave night, not a single princess gliding
Through secret forests, enchanting deer and
Butterflies with her smile...... What a pleasure
to be wrong. Princesses, knights, enchantments and
dragons, mystery and adventure .....not only are they
here-and-now, they're all that ever lived on earth![38]

— RICHARD BACH

In our modern age, romantic love is still the theme of many forms of art and entertainment. Popular culture, as it is expresses through films and music is rich with romantic love. While romantic love is still the dream of many, some claim that the more modern presentations of the media are still not realistic. Romantic love, as depicted in books and movies, is thought to be extremely rare and may not ever occur at all. Critics point at the modern dating practices in which sex is really the only true goal of the partners and a lasting relationship is almost never the case. Many people also suggest that the rigorous demands of money and careers often rob people of the romantic ideal and that the wider vision of love can never be realized.

MODERN DAY DRAGONS

Modern statistics and the many observations of psychologists also paint a somewhat dim picture about romantic love. Although love is certainly thought to be a reality that is possible in our age, it is often represented in the mass media as something other than realistic. The dragons of the modern age may still be alive and well but their imaginary quality may now come to us in a completely different way. Many argue that the modern day dragons are intimately connected to the mass media in the way that it presents love as a romantic fantasy rather than a higher level of spiritual awareness.

Love as depicted in the mass media is not what this level is about. What the world generally refers to as 'love' is an intense emotional condition, combining physical attraction, possessiveness,

control, addiction, eroticism and novelty. It's usually
fragile and fluctuating, waxing and waning with
varying conditions.[39]

— Hawkins

It may certainly be that love is still a realistic goal to obtain in our lives but many of the false ideas about romantic love may have to first be addressed if we are to overcome its obstacles in the modern age. We may need a new way of looking at romantic love that will help us to find our true destiny and a lasting relationship. Hidden underneath the temporary attractiveness of the common romantic notions will hopefully lie an attention to our own spiritual practices and a more serious concern for the law of attraction.

Growth in Relationships

As the attraction to the higher levels of awareness intensifies in our lives, an underlying vibration will become the glue that holds a relationship together. Attraction becomes more than just a temporary relationship between two people but rather a balancing force that continues to make each partner attractive to the other. The individuals move out into the world and begin to establish relationships in their careers and social lives so that they learn to practice the principles of love with everyone they meet. This is a further advancement in awareness that could be understood as the tendency toward unconditional love.

Love is often considered to be a power that can endure for eternity because it strives toward a unity between all things rather than just two people. This eternal nature is also a tendency toward unconditional love as it incorporates not only the two individuals who were first attracted to each other but others whom they meet after they have first fallen in love. Growing couples learn to share their love with the others around them and move forward toward a more eternal vision of love. The tendency toward unconditional love may begin when a couple decides to move forward as individuals, either in their careers or in the case of a family.

FAMILY

Starting a family has always been the natural progression that a couple in love will embark upon. Just like the challenges they first face in their romantic love, the challenges they face with children are often profoundly underestimated. A mother and father must endure many more responsibilities than they ever imagined and arguments over how to raise the children are often at the top of the list when it comes to disagreements between spouses. The law of attraction applies here just as it has applied in every circumstance before. We become what we think about as individuals and as a family.

It is interesting to see the way children often take on very different roles from their parents. They have minds of their own and there really is no way of controlling them. In the same way that couples tend to create a balance between them, families also tend to move toward a balance and various roles will come into play so as to carry on this underlying vibration of wholeness and totality in the family. It is important to remember that we can only control the small things but not the big things. Family members will all have different visions of what is right for them and we must be open to the individual differences of each person. If the par-

ents are to continue to strive for the higher level of awareness that they reached in their own relationship, they will
have to continue to apply this to their children who eventually introduce new challenges to the family dynamic. It
seems as though the original idea that opposites attract
would be showing its colors once again and yet a family will
not stay together unless there is an underlying set of values
which hold the entire unit together.

Family patterns and family structure have changed alot
in the past few decades. However, it is still a great advantage
for children if they are encouraged to pursue positive and
worthwhile values in their everyday lives. Some of the more
basic core values that help to promote a positive attractiveness are the pursuit of personal development, independence
and responsibility, leadership, citizenship, respect for others
and a positive enjoyment of life.

In the case of personal development, children should be
encouraged to develop physically, emotionally and mental-
ly. They should learn positive values that are related to their
health, learning, creativity and exploration. These may
include the ability to trust themselves and others through the
use of open communication and genuine concern. Healthy
competition that springs from a mutual support can also be
emphasized. These attractive values help to contribute to the
positive development of any individual and they are essential to promoting a better quality of life.

In terms of independence, a child should be provided
with an individual sense of freedom but should also learn
personal responsibility and self-control. Activities that allow
them to act independently and responsibly will encourage an
attractiveness toward these values in greater proportions

over time. Parents should allow children to make mistakes and then to learn from those mistakes. The children can learn to become involved in the planning and execution of their own future in a manner that promotes their own independence and personal responsibility.

Leadership is also an important value to promote in the family as it is closely tied to independence and responsibility. Many experts believe that leadership qualities emerge naturally as long as parents promote the values of being positive and enjoying the many opportunities that life has to offer. Parents can reinforce these ideals, however, by modelling the more positive and constructive values in their own families.

Citizenship is a higher level value that children can benefit from as it helps them to recognize the value of the democratic process and their own role as a citizen in a democracy. Parents should recognize that their opinions, ideas and values will strongly affect the perceptions of their children and eventually affect their overall attitude about their own careers and work ethic in the larger community.

Learning to respect others is probably one of the most important values that children can benefit from as it teaches them how to become attractive and to ultimately love another person. Respect is intimately connected to responsibility. Our responsibility to each other is what makes our relationships both lasting and loving. Children can learn that it is their own responsibility to see their behavior as having an impact upon others in either a positive or negative way and this will teach them to develop better relationships.

Finally, a positive enjoyment of life is probably the most central value that a child can learn. Life can be seen as great! It can have adventures, surprises and lots of joy. Eventually they may become leaders who inspire others by the way they perceive life. Problems can be seen as challenges to be overcome and as positive learning experiences rather than permanent obstacles.

By incorporating the many values already mentioned and others such as courtesy, acceptance, compassion and integrity, a family will become an attractive field of spiritual values where the members can thrive and grow. The law of attraction can be implemented in a positive way for both individuals and families so as to bring about a healthy manner of living.

– PART V –

HEALTH

*A*pplying the law of attraction to our physical bodies is probably one of the most common applications that people use. We commonly think of attraction as something that has to do with personal appearance and we associate a healthy body with an attractive person. Maintaining our health will certainly make us more attractive and will also promote more positive thoughts and emotions. A healthy body leads to a healthy state of mind and maintaining these two things is all part of a positive spiritual approach.

NUTRITION

Nutrition is one of the most important elements of maintaining a strong body. A positive attitude toward nutrition will attract more information into your life about better and easier diets so that eventually your daily eating habits will become effortless. It is extremely important to have a good diet that will ensure the proper ratio of macro and micronutrients in the daily regimen. This nutritional concern will aid the body in its recovery process after a strenuous exercise and also maintain a general level of health and well being. Adhering to a low-intake diet takes a lot of the stress off the bodies internal functions and makes it a lot easier to maintain a healthy weight over time. This is just another example of the law of attraction taking effect in our lives.

EXERCISE

Physical exercise is also one of the most highly recommended ways of achieving a good overall health in the body. This can be focused in various athletic abilities or just a regular physical exercise. Whichever method we choose, it is proven that physical exercise is paramount in the prevention of many diseases such as cancer, diabetes, cardiovascular disease, and obesity.

Exercises can be divided into three groups; flexibility exercises, aerobic exercises and anaerobic exercises. As we learn more about each form of exercise, we will also be presented with more opportunities to improve and widen our horizons in the xercise world. Flexibility exercises include the stretching of the muscles and joints to improve flexibility while aerobic exercises include walking, running or swimming to increase the cardiovascular endurance. Anaerobic exercises include more rigorous muscle exercises such as weight training or sprinting to increase the strength of the muscles. Physical exercise helps a person to maintain a healthy weight, healthy bones, muscles, and joints and promotes overall physiological and psychological well-being It also increases the strength of the immune system and may prevent the need for surgery or other invasive medical procedures down the road.

Exercise has been proven to aid in proper brain function by increasing the flow of the blood and oxygen to the brain. It also increases the growth factor of nerve cells in the body by increasing the chemicals that are needed for cognition. The active breathing that takes place during exercise can help to increase a person's lung capacity and oxygen intake. This brings about a greater cardiac efficiency because the heart will do less work when it has to oxygenate the muscles. Conscious deep breathing during aerobic exercise will help to develop heart and lung efficiency. All of these things work together to promote further advantages to our overall health and to give us even greater opportunities down the road.

YOGA

Yoga is a Sanscrit term meaning "union". It is an ancient spiritual practice that began in India thousands of years ago where it is still practiced as a great tradition. There are many forms of yoga such as Karma, Bhakti, Jnana and Raja, but in the West it has become more associated with various postures and fitness exercises which can eventually lead to a more advanced form of relaxation.

Yoga is a practice which certainly adheres to the law of attraction in that its advocates develop greater and greater expertise and eventually become attracted to the most advanced forms of yoga. These more advanced forms are practiced in the form of deep meditation and the ultimate experience of Samadhi or Enlightenment. It is said that the energies which an advanced student obtains from yoga will eventually and spontaneously attract the experience of Enlightenment through their own inherent powers and this is the ultimate goal of yoga. As a way of achieving Enlightenment, yoga is considered to be an essential part of both Hinduism and Buddhism and has also spread to many other religions around the world.

Traditional yogic techniques not only incorporate stretching and breathing exercises but typically include moral and ethical principles and a spiritual philosophy similar to that which is contained in the law of attraction itself. We call those energies toward ourselves which we meditate on everyday and this is basically an advanced application of the law of attraction. Eventually students may find themselves attracted to the specific teachings of a guru and may find themselves chanting specific mantras such as the sound "Om" which is considered by many enlightened masters to be the sacred sound of the universe.

Many people now see yoga as a daily practice that is beneficial because it leads to an improved health, emotional balance, clarity of thought and a joy of life. Students of yoga may also be attracted to several breathing exercises and a stilling of the mind through the technique of meditation and this is merely a more focused aspect of the many yogic practices.

MEDITATION

Meditation is a specific element of yoga which generally involves the turning of a person's attention inward to the workings of their own mind and thoughts. It encompasses a lot of different spiritual practices but generally focuses on the mental activity and an achievement of internal peace. Many practitioners of meditation see it as a great way to become friendlier and healthier in their own lives.

A derivative of meditation which is more commonly practiced in the Christian religion is that of contemplation where the mind is encouraged to reflect upon certain ideas so as to bring it into a more harmonious alignment with healthier attitudes and directions. An example of Christian contemplation might be the contemplation of the sufferings of Christ. Generally speaking, however, meditation tends to be a practice which focuses the mind on a single object or idea such as the breath or a sacred mantra. By practicing meditation, people become better at opening up to the powers of the divine and these powers become even more attractive as they develop inside each person.

– Part VI –

Conclusions

he law of attraction is a profound truth that has been passed down to us through the teachings of the Buddha and through numerous other spiritual traditions throughout history. It has been explained to us that our actions don't just have an effect in this life but in future lives and that this is the reason for our fortunes and our sorrows each minute. Even science has shown us that the power of attraction is extremely significant in every aspect of our lives and is akin to the very glue which holds the entire universe together. If we wish to harness the immense strength of this power of attraction, it can only be through our own will that we strive to change our direction and enter into a larger field of attraction which can bring a more comprehensive experience of joy and happiness in our lives.

"As ye sow, so shall ye reap" is offered to us both as Christians and Buddhists alike, and Earl Nightengale has given us a modern wake-up call to this pervasive truth in his "Strange Secret" philosophy. He has aptly told us "We become what we think about" and indeed, this law of attraction is becoming more and more understood each day. As we advance forward and come to know the great powers that lie within our own consciousness we learn that they only need to be unlocked in order that they reach their fullest potential. Once this happens, the "Strange Secret" that Nightengale speaks of may no longer be a secret and there may be nothing strange about it to anyone.

References

[1] Unknown, Josephson Institute of Ethics, josephsoninstitute.org.

[2] Buddha, *How Karma Works: The Twelve Links of Dependent-Arising*, by Geshe Sonam Rinchen.

[3] Luke 6: 37.

[4] Earl Nightengale, *The Strangest Secret*, Millennium 2000 Gold Record Recording (Audio CD).

[5] Clark, John, O.E. (2004). The Essential Dictionary of Science. Barnes & Noble Books.

[6] Cline, David B., "The Search for Dark Matter," *Scientific American*, March 2003.

[7] Michael Moncur's Collection of Quotations, September 23, 2006, www.quotationspage.com.

[8] Alice Bailey, *The Consciousness of the Atom*, 1922.

[9] Dr. David R. Hawkins, *Power Versus Force*, 1995, Veritas Publishing, p. 90.

[10] *A Course in Miracles,* Foundation for Inner Peace, p. 20.

[11] Peter Mertvago, ed., *Dictionary of 1000 German Proverbs*, New York: Hippocrene Books.

[12] A. Koestler, *The Ghost in the Machine*, 1967.

[13] Deepak Chopra, *The Path to Love: Spiritual Strategies for Healing*, Harper Collins, 1993.

[14] Napoleon Hill, *Think and Grow Rich: The Andrew Carnegie Formula for Money Making*, Random House, 1960.

[15] Shakti Gawain, *Creative Visualization: Use the Power of Your Imagination to Create What You Want in Your Life*, Nataraj Publishing, 2002.

[16] Collection of Proverbs, josephsoninstitute.org.

[17] *A Course in Miracles*, Foundation for Inner Peace, p.1.

18 Eckhart Tolle, *The Power of Now*, 2001.

19 Peter Ouspensky, *A New Model of the Universe: Principles of the Psychological Method in its Application to Problems of Science, Religion and Art*, 1931.

20 Dr. David R. Hawkins, *The Eye of the Eye*, Veritas Publishing, 2000.

21 Dr. David R. Hawkins, *I, Reality and Subjectivity*, Veritas Publishing, 2002.

22 Dr. David R. Hawkins, *The Eye of the Eye*, Veritas Publishing, 2000, p. 125.

23 Dr. David R. Hawkins, *Power Versus Force*, 1995, p. 29.

24 Lao Tzu, *The Tao Te Ching of Lao Tzu*, translated by Brian Browne Walker, 2001.

25 Lao Tzu, *The Tao Te Ching of Lao Tzu*, translated by Brian Browne Walker, 2001

26 Lao Tzu, *The Tao Te Ching of Lao Tzu*, translated by Brian Browne Walker, 2001

27 Johan Wolfgang von Goethe, *Conversations of Goethe*, Johan Peter Eckerman, First Da Capo Hit, 1998.

28 Dr. David R. Hawkins, *Power Versus Force*, Veritas Publishing, 1995, p. 263.

29 1 Timothy 6:10.

30 Matthew 6: 27, 34.

31 Dr. David R. Hawkins, *I, Reality and Subjectivity*, Veritas Publishing, 2002, pp. 33-34.

32 Dale Carnegie,

33 John H. Holland, *Emergence from Chaos to Order*, Oxford University Press, 1998.

34 Wayne Dyer, *Inspiration: Your Ultimate Calling*, Hay House, 2006.

35 Thomas Kostigen, CBS.MarketWatch.com, "Reaching New Heights: What Money Means to Donald Trump."

36 Earl Nightengale, *The Strangest Secret*, Millennium 2000 Gold Record Recording (Audio CD).

37 e. e. cummings, *100 Selected Poems by e.e. cummings*

Works Cited

Bach, Richard. *The Bridge Across Forever.* Dell Publishing, 1984.

Bailey, Alice. *The Consciousness of the Atom.* 1922.

Bible, King James Version.

Carnegie, Dale. *How to Win Friends & Influence People.* Pocket Books, 1936.

Chopra, Deepak. *The Path to Love: Spiritual Strategies for Healing.* Harper Collins, 1993.

Clark, John. *The Essential Dictionary of Science.* Barnes & Noble Books.

Cline, David B. "The Search for Dark Matter," *Scientific American.* March 2003

Cummings, E. E. *100 Selected Poems by E. E. Cummings.* Grove Hit, 1954

Dyer, Wayne. *Inspiration: Your Ultimate Calling.* Hay House, 2006.

Gawain, Shakti. *Creative Visualization: Use the Power of Your Imagination to Create What You Want in Your Life.* Nataraj Publishing, 2002.

Goethe, Johan Wolfgang von. *Conversations of Goethe with Johan Peter Eckerman,* trans. John Oxenford. First Da Capo Hit, 1998.

Hawkins, Dr. David R. *The Eye of the Eye.* Veritas Publishing, 2000

Hawkins, Dr. David R. *I, Reality and Subjectivity.* Veritas Publishing, 2002.

Hawkins, Dr. David R. *Power Versus Force.* Veritas Publishing, 1995.

Hill, Napoleon. *Think and Grow Rich: The Andrew Carnegie Formula for Money Making.* Random House, 1960.

Holland, John H. *Emergence from Chaos to Order.* Oxford University Press, 1998.

Josephson Institute. *Collection of Proverbs.* Josephsoninstitute.*org*

Kostigen, Thomas. "Reaching New Heights: What Money Means to

Donald Trump," CBS.MarketWatch.com

Lao Tzu. *The Tao Te Ching of Lao Tzu,* trans. Brian Browne Walker. St. Martin's Griffin, 2001.

Mertvago, Peter, ed. *Dictionary of 1000 German Proverbs.* New York: Hippocrene Books.

Moncur, Michael. Quotation #1388 from Michael Moncur's (Cynical) Quotations. www.quotationspage.com

Nightingale, Earl. *The Strangest Secret.* Millennium 2000 Gold Record Recording (Audio CD).

Ouspensky, Peter. *A New Model of the Universe.* 1931.

Tolle, Eckhart. *The Power of Now, 2001*

Also Available from *Guide for Living*: